Red squirrels

Naturally Scottish

Scottish Natural Heritage
Dualchas Nàdair na h-Alba
All of nature for all of Scotland
Nàdar air fad airson Alba air fad

Author: Peter Lurz
Contributions from: Mairi Cole (SNH)
Series Editor: John Baxter (SNH)
Design and production: SNH Publishing

www.snh.org.uk

© Scottish Natural Heritage 2010

Photography: Uno Berggren/Ardea.com 17; **Niall Benvie/Images from the edge** 22, 26 left, 41; **Trevor Bryan/Alamy** 20; **Laurie Campbell** frontispiece, 16 left, 33 top, 35, 44 left, 46&47; **Laurie Campbell/SNH** 19 top; **Pete Cairns/Northshots** 2, 12&13, 18, 26&27; **Bruce Dunlop** 47 right; **NHPA/Photoshot/Suzanne Danegger** 31; **NHPA/Photoshot/Gerard Lacz** 32; **David Everest, Veterinary Laboratories Agency** 34; **Forestry Commission Picture Library** 43; **Forestry Commission Picture Library/Fort Augustus FD** 40 bottom; **Forestry Commission Picture Library/Isobel Cameron** 40 top; **Lorne Gill/SNH** inside front & inside back cover, opposite foreword, opposite introduction, 15 right, 16 top right, 21 top left, 21 top right, 21 bottom left, 21 bottom right, 36, 37; **Mark Hamblin** 23, 33 bottom, 48**; Imagebroker/Alamy** 10, 30; **Neil McIntyre** front cover, contents, 6, 7, 11, 14&15, 24&25, 28, 42, 44&45; **NHPA/Bence Mate** 19 bottom; **Roger Powell/NaturePL** 38&39; **Keith Ringland** 3 right; **Samphoto** 16 bottom right; **AlanWilliams/NHPA/Photoshot** 3 left.

Illustration: Ashworth Maps Interpretation Ltd 4, 5; **Keith Brockie** 8, 9; **Clare Hewitt** 29; **Kelly Stuart/SNH** 38.

ISBN: 978 1 85397 601 8
S1K0610

Further copies are available from: Publications,
Scottish Natural Heritage, Battleby, Redgorton, Perth PH1 3EW
Tel 01738 458530 Fax 01738 456613 pubs@snh.gov.uk

This publication is printed on Revive 75.
This paper contains material sourced from responsibly managed and sustainable forests certified in accordance with the FSC (Forestry Stewardship Council).

Further booklets in the series are available. To order these and other publications visit: snh.org.uk/pubs

Front cover image:
Red squirrel on trunk of oak tree, Cairngorms National Park.
Frontispiece:
Red squirrel.
Inside front cover:
Remnants of pine cones eaten by red squirrels.

Red squirrels

Naturally Scottish

by Peter Lurz

Foreword

The red squirrel is one of the most popular species of mammal in Britain, coming second in a Government poll of species judged to be most important to the Scottish people. It has been portrayed as emblematic, charismatic and iconic and, in my view, it warrants all of these descriptions. Although timid creatures, red squirrels are easily recognisable in their woodland home and we are fortunate in Scotland to have many places where we can enjoy seeing them as part of our countryside.

The species has a long and complex history in Britain. Populations have not always been stable and, although they have persisted through good and bad times, they are once again facing great challenges to their survival. However, Scotland has an estimated 75% of the UK's population and, consequently, we can also offer the greatest hope for the future of the species in the UK. We are meeting these challenges in Government through the inclusion of the red squirrel under Scotland's Biodiversity Strategy and as one of 32 priority species on the Species Action Framework. This action is fully matched by partners to Government, who continue to demonstrate a strong commitment to conserving the species in Scotland. Government could not meet the challenges without this support and we are now in a great position of being able to ask not "What can be done?" for the species but "Who will do what, and when?"

The key message of the Scotland's Biodiversity Strategy is "It's in Your Hands". Never has this been a more appropriate sentiment than for red squirrel conservation and I hope you find this book informative and that it instils an enthusiasm to help conserve this fascinating creature.

Roseanna Cunningham MSP
Minister for Environment

1
Red squirrel, one of Scotland's most well-loved mammals.

1

Contents

1
Red squirrels spend a considerable time on the ground foraging for food.

1

1
Mixed deciduous and conifer woodland, Dunkeld, Perthshire.

Introduction

The red squirrel *Sciurus vulgaris,* is one of our most popular and well-loved mammals. Archaeological remains of the species date back approximately 8,700 years although squirrels are accepted by experts to have been in Britain from the end of the last Ice Age (between 12,500 and 10,000 years ago). They arrived in the south, from Europe, and spread north as tundra and ice was replaced by woodland habitats. Although they lived across much of the British Isles, populations have not always been stable. Extensive areas of woodland have been lost due to large-scale deforestation to make way for agriculture, as well as a huge demand for wood for industrial purposes, and red squirrel populations were reported to be extinct in many parts of Scotland by the 18th century. Red squirrels were re-introduced from England, and possibly continental Europe, in the late 18th and early 19th centuries to augment these losses, with the most notable releases at Dalkeith (Midlothian), Dunkeld (Perthshire), Arbroath (Forfar), Minto (Roxburgh), Haining (Borders), Beaufort Castle (Highland) and Minard (Argyll).

The remaining red squirrel population began to thrive alongside introduced ones following large-scale planting of conifer species in the late 18th and 19th centuries. Red squirrels subsequently became so numerous that they were considered a woodland pest by some forest managers in the late 19th century, because of the damage they caused to trees. As a result of this, they were controlled across many estates in Scotland (see also section on 'Squirrels and people').

Background

The red squirrel faces a new threat from the introduced North American grey squirrel, *Sciurus carolinensis.* This species was first released in England, in 1876, at Henbury Park in Cheshire. It has a similar lifestyle to the red squirrel and competes for resources such as food and shelter sites. It has replaced the red squirrel throughout most of mainland England and Wales, although red squirrels can still be found in small pockets of Lancashire, Yorkshire and County Durham, as well as parts of Cumbria and Northumberland. Red squirrels also still live on the Isle of White, Brownsea and Furzey in Poole Harbour as well as Northern Ireland, although their range there has contracted noticeably since the introduction of grey squirrels at Castles Forbes in 1913.

In Scotland, the grey squirrel was released in three places: Argyll (1892), Fife (1919) and Edinburgh. The precise date of their release in Edinburgh is not recorded but there were sightings at Corstorphine by 1913 and at Dalmeny Park in 1919. They spread rapidly from these places and were commonly found throughout the central belt by 1955. They subsequently spread south into the Borders and north into Perthshire and Deeside, and were first recorded in Aberdeen in the 1970s. This is believed to have been the result of a deliberate introduction.

Grey squirrels are now widespread in Scotland. They continue to spread more widely and, as in England and Wales, they have replaced the native red squirrel as they spread. Red squirrels do co-exist with grey squirrels in some areas on the edge of their range, however, and are still abundant in places where the grey squirrel is absent, especially in the north of Scotland (see pages 4 and 5).

1

1
Grey squirrel in Princes Street Gardens, Edinburgh. Grey squirrels are a common sight in many public parks and towns.
2
Grey squirrel.
3
Red squirrel.

2

3

Map showing red squirrel distribution 2006–2007

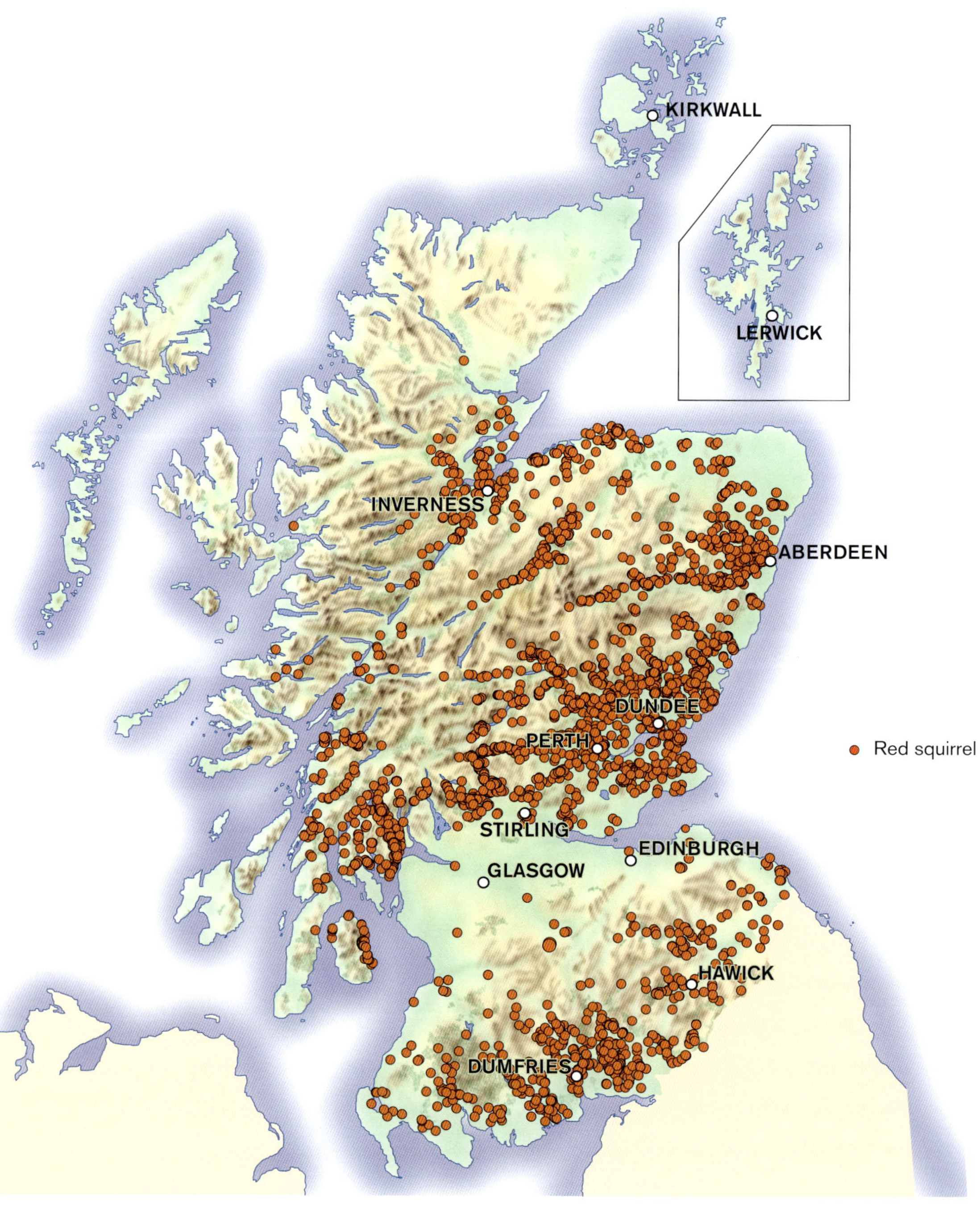

Map showing grey squirrel distribution 2006–2007

Identifying squirrels

Squirrels are rodents. They belong to the family Sciurudae, which includes gliding, tree and ground-dwelling squirrel species. Both red and grey squirrels are 'tree squirrels' and are two of 27 species of tree squirrels in the genus *Sciurus*. There are a total of 81 species of tree squirrels described worldwide. Fossil evidence, based on bone length and jaw structure, suggests that tree squirrels evolved from more primitive rodents at the end of the Eocene period, about 36 million years ago.

Squirrels are well suited to living in woodland habitats, having large eyes, relatively small ears and long hind limbs adapted for leaping. Their amazing ability to turn their hind feet through 180° gives them a strong grip and allows them move down a tree head first.

Male and female red squirrels are approximately the same size, typically weighing between 270 and 360 grams. Fur colour can vary markedly from almost black to chestnut or light brown on the back, and from white to cream on the chest and stomach. Red squirrels moult twice a year, with fur replaced from the head along the body to the flanks in the spring and, in reverse from the flanks towards the head in autumn. The ear tufts and tail moult once, with hair replaced in late summer and autumn. Ear tufts thin out and often are completely absent in the summer.

Only red squirrels have ear tufts and these bleach in colour, becoming almost blonde from June onwards.

1

1
Red squirrel in summer showing an absence of ear tufts, collecting pine cones.
2
Red squirrel showing characteristic ear tufts and white chest and stomach.

2

Red squirrel

Size: 18–24 centimetres long (head and body)

Grey squirrel

Size: 24–28 centimetres long (head and body)

The ear tufts and tail of some red squirrels bleach from winter to summer, becoming blonde, or even white, from June onwards. It was suggested in the 18th century that this represented a different subspecies and was given the name *Sciurus vulgaris leucourus.* Subsequent studies have not been able to confirm this, although pilot studies have found unique red squirrel genotypes in some regions in the UK, such as Cumbria and Wales.

Grey squirrels are much heavier than red squirrels, with fully-grown adult males reaching up to 720 grams. The body is predominantly grey coloured, with some brown on the flanks and back. Bellies may be white, grey to buff or cinnamon in colour. The tail appears grey, banded with brown or black. Long, white-tipped guard hairs may give the appearance of a halo around the tail.

Melanistic ('black' squirrels) examples of both red and grey squirrels can occur. These are usually associated with mountainous areas and, in the case of red squirrels, are more common in the north-eastern part of its European range. 'Black' grey squirrels are more common in the northern part of its native North American range. In the UK, dark red squirrels have been reported in Argyll and 'black grey squirrels' from Cambridgeshire.

The large variability in coat colour means that this is not always a reliable way to distinguish red squirrels from grey squirrels, especially if only a fleeting glimpse is caught amongst the trees. However, only red squirrels have striking ear tufts, between 2 and 3.5 centimetres long, from autumn to spring.

Red squirrels have an amazing ability to rotate their hind feet 180° to move down trees head first.

3

3
Melanistic red squirrel.

4
A red squirrel defying gravity due to its ability to rotate its hind feet.

4

Habitat

Red squirrels are found in most woodland habitats, from conifer forests to broadleaf woods and copses. They are commonly seen in urban parks and gardens where grey squirrels are not present. Although generally considered to prefer conifer habitats, red squirrels survive well in both conifer and broadleaf woodland, particularly those with plentiful hazel nuts. However, they do not compete well with grey squirrels in areas of large-seeded broadleaf (e.g. oak woodland) and, under these conditions, the number of red squirrels will reduce until the population is lost, generally within 15 years of grey squirrels appearing in the area.

Red squirrel distribution is influenced by the kind of trees and shrubs present, as well as their age. Trees have to be old enough to produce seeds as this determines the type of foods available to them. In general, red squirrels fare better in areas with a variety of tree species. This is due to the seeding patterns of trees. Most tree species have years when an abundance of seeds are produced (mast crops) followed by years with average or poor seeding. Different tree species do not mast in the same years and a good year for one species of tree can be a poor year for another. Woodland composed of a mixture of species will, therefore, provide a more dependable supply of seed food for squirrels.

Red squirrels generally live within a home range which varies according to the season, habitat type and the abundance and quality of food.

1
Red squirrels favour conifer forest where there is a plentiful food supply.

2

3

Grey squirrels originated in broadleaf forests in North America and generally out compete red squirrels in these habitats in the UK. They are considered to be broadleaf specialists although they can live in conifer forests, including pine woods, at lower densities. Grey squirrels living in conifer habitats have a lower fecundity (i.e. fewer females breeding and fewer young) and higher mortality rates than grey squirrels in deciduous habitats. However, the presence of large-seeded broadleaf trees, particularly beech, oak and chestnut, within or near conifer forests can improve conditions and enable them to increase their population densities.

In areas where grey squirrels are present, red squirrels will persist longest where there is conifer habitat. Consequently, conservation efforts focus heavily on maximising the area of conifer woodlands available to support strong red squirrel populations which can outcompete grey squirrels in the long-term (see Threats and conservation).

Red squirrels fare better in woodlands with a variety of tree species.

2
Red squirrel feeding on oak buds.
3
Loch of the Lowes, Dunkeld.

Nesting

Both red and grey squirrel nests (called 'dreys') consist of an outer shell of twigs along with a soft, insulating inner core of mosses, leaves, conifer needles and grass. Dreys are usually near the main trunk of the tree and are supported by branches. However, in the north-west of Scotland, where there are pine martens present, dreys appear to be more commonly found out on branches, where they are more difficult for the pine marten to reach.

Red squirrels also use open platforms of twigs and softer material, or sheltered, disused bird nests for resting in summer. Breeding dreys, in which they look after their young, are usually larger and may be lined with soft grass clippings. Red squirrels tend to use more than one drey at any given time. Individuals have been known to use as many as eight dreys for resting during the day and sleeping at night, although the average is three. Some of these dreys may also be used by other squirrels at different times. Red squirrels will sometimes live together in dreys during the winter.

Counting the number of dreys that can be seen within a deciduous wood in autumn can provide rough estimate of the number of squirrels present. By measuring this over a specified area, for example one hectare, this can provide a crude estimate of squirrel density. Information on how to do this is available under 'Further reading'.

2

3

1

Red squirrels may use an average of three dreys at any one time.

1
Squirrel drey.

2
Lichen and moss are used to line squirrel dreys.

3
Red squirrel collecting lichen for drey building.

4
Red squirrel drey inside a hollow tree – dreys provide a safe and warm environment in which squirrels rear their young.

4

1

2

Diet

Red squirrels have a varied diet. Seeds of deciduous and conifer tree species are the most important food, although they also eat other plant material such as fruit, tree shoots, buds, bark and even lichens. Fruits eaten by red squirrels in Scotland include rose hips, blackberries, raspberries and bilberries. Contrary to popular belief, both red and grey squirrels will eat hazel nuts while they are green.

1
Red squirrel foraging for hazel nuts.

2
Pine seedling.

3
Red squirrels obtain most of their water from their food but occasionally drink from pools.

3

4

Fungi can be an important food source in years when seeds are scarce. Studies on the stomach contents of red squirrels in Russia estimated that 63% of the diet consisted of tree seeds, 25% of fungi and 12% of buds and willow catkins. Squirrels can also play an important role in forest ecology by dispersing the spores of truffle-like fungi, which they dig up and eat.

Red squirrels may also take songbird eggs and chicks, and insects, if the opportunity arises. Bones and antlers are sometimes found on the forest floor with squirrel teeth marks on them. These may be gnawed to sharpen and trim incisor teeth and to obtain calcium. Squirrels get their water either from food or from surface water such as dew, although they are known to drink from streams or ponds during dry spells in the summer.

In autumn mushrooms can be seen placed on branches up trees. Closer examination will reveal incisor marks along the stem where the squirrel carried it with its teeth. They put them there to dry and then store them in little larders called 'scatter hoards'. *Boletus* is a favourite mushroom species although less palatable fungi such as the red-coloured Sickener *Russula emetica*, are also known to be taken.

Squirrels hang their mushrooms out to dry on branches of trees.

5

6

7

8

4
Mushrooms are an important addition to a squirrel's diet in the autumn months.

A squirrel's varied diet includes:
5
Rose hips,
6
Mushrooms,
7
Pine cones,
8
Brambles.

Caching

Red squirrels are 'scatter hoarders', meaning that they store seeds and other food items in different locations. They spend a significant amount of time storing food during the autumn, when it is abundant, using holes just under the surface of the soil or leaf litter, tree hollows or their drey. Caching food is very important for them and retrieved food can support them through spells of severe weather or periods of food shortage.

In areas where grey and red squirrels overlap, grey squirrels are known to pilfer the food stored by red squirrels in late winter and spring. It is argued that the loss of this important food source at this critical time has the potential to affect breeding success in red squirrels. The scale of such pilfering and whether red squirrels also steal from grey squirrels has still to be established.

Caught red-handed – squirrels often steal food stored by other squirrels.

1
Food stores are important to help squirrels survive the lean times.

2
Red squirrels will happily exploit other food sources given the chance.

1

2

Social organisation, space use and activity patterns

Social organisation in red squirrels depends largely on the distribution of resources such as food, nesting sites and mates.

Squirrels generally restrict their daily activity to a measurable 'home range', which varies according to season, habitat type and the abundance and quality of food available. Neither males nor females are territorial and their home ranges overlap extensively with those of other males and females. Older females may, however, exclude other individuals from their nest areas during the breeding season. Home ranges vary between 2.8 and 6.8 hectares for deciduous woods, and between 7 and 23 hectares for conifer woodlands. Summer ranges tend to be larger than winter ranges.

Squirrels adapt their foraging behaviour according to the type of food available and home ranges. For example, food may become scarce in spring or early summer in conifer woodlands when autumn tree seed crops become exhausted. This causes an increase in home range size as the animals forage further afield to find suitable food. Squirrels will also adjust where they forage within a wood according to the season. Seeds and fruits are generally available in the canopy of broadleaf woods only between August and early November, and squirrels will forage for fallen seeds on the ground during winter. When seeds are scarce, red squirrels also rely more heavily on alternative food sources such as fungi, buds or shoots, as well as their cached food. If food sources fail completely, both adults and juveniles may disperse from the area to find alternative supplies.

Neither red nor grey squirrels hibernate, but they are less active in winter, usually for only a few hours each day at first light. They may even remain in their dreys during bad weather. In spring, daily activity is extended as seasonal daylight and temperature increase. From May to October they are active during two periods in a day: one in the morning and, after a rest period, another in the afternoon.

1

1
Where food is plentiful it is possible to see more than one red squirrel at a time.

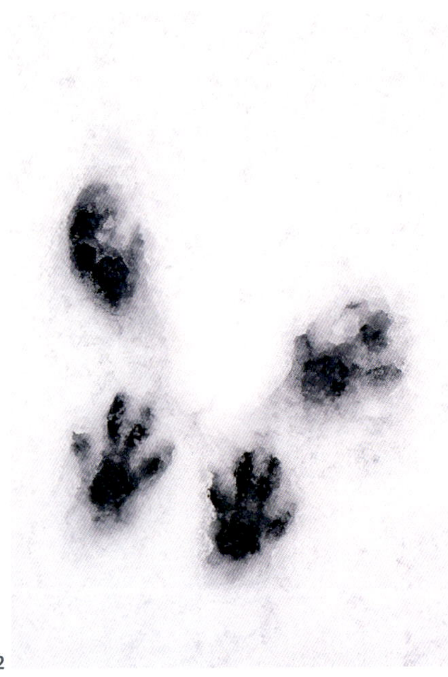

2

2
Often the only indication of the presence of red squirrels in winter is their footprints in the snow.

3
The red squirrel must forage even in extreme cold as it cannot survive for more than a few days without food.

3

1

Life history, breeding and annual cycles

Squirrel breeding seasons vary from year to year and are linked to the body condition and weight of individuals. In the UK, red squirrels have to exceed 280–300 grams to come into breeding condition, with females in areas with a good food supply giving birth to heavier young which, in turn, are more likely to be weaned successfully.

Red squirrels become sexually active at about nine to ten months of age. In Scotland mating can start as early as December and continue until July. Gestation lasts between 36 and 42 days and young are weaned at about eight to ten weeks. Red squirrels can have one or two litters per year, with spring litters born in February or March and summer litters in May or June. Breeding success depends on food availability, weather and individual body conditions, hence not all females will breed twice. Females in their first breeding year breed only once (see diagram below). Litter size varies and can range between one and six young, although the average red squirrel litter size is three or four.

In 2008 a record litter of seven young (one female and six males) was confirmed from a mountain pine habitat in northern Italy. There have previously been anecdotal reports of large litters in red squirrels but the Italian litter illustrates the huge reproductive potential of squirrels.

Annual Breeding Cycle – variation between years can be expected

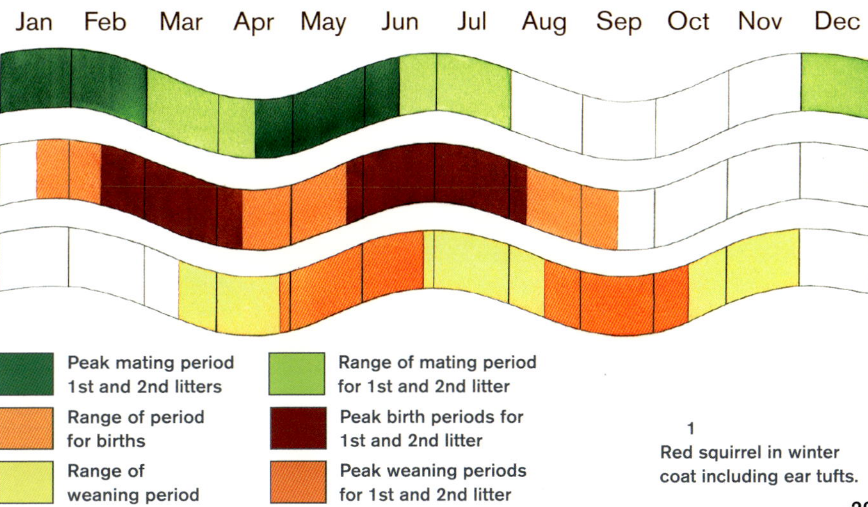

1
Red squirrel in winter coat including ear tufts.

2

3

Females living in areas with good food supplies give birth to heavier young which are, in turn, more likely to be weaned successfully.

2
Family of young red squirrels in a nest of moss and pine needles.
3
Young squirrels need to practise their balancing.

Males are reproductively active for most of breeding season and do not share in caring for the young. Females come into heat for only one day during each oestrous cycle and there is little courtship prior to mating. A 'mating chase' may be observed in which several males follow a female in heat. Behavioural studies suggest that the heaviest, or most dominant, male accounts for most matings, although other males may 'sneak' in to mate as an alternative strategy.

The availability of food in the environment has a strong influence on the survival of both adult and young red squirrels. An estimated 15–25% of juveniles may survive their first winter, with the survival rate of these animals subsequently increasing to approximately 50%. Red squirrels surviving their first year may have an average life expectancy of about three to four years in the wild, with some animals living to six or seven years. Life expectancy in captive animals can be longer (up to ten years).

Predators and disease

A range of predators are known to kill red squirrels. Mammal predators include wild and domestic cats, pine martens, foxes and polecats. Stoats have been observed to take nestlings, and dogs will chase and take a squirrel if they can catch it. Large raptors, such as goshawks and some species of owl, also take red squirrels. However, there is no evidence to support the suggestion that any of these predators has a significant role in the national decline of the species.

Red squirrels also suffer on our roads. Black spots have been identified on some roads around the country where, usually due to dispersal movements between woodlands, high numbers of red squirrels are killed. Rope bridges can be erected to provide an alternative route.

Squirrels can carry a variety of external and internal parasites. Some of these may be benign whilst some may cause disease. Like most wild mammals, they carry ticks, lice and fleas. One species of flea carried by red squirrels on the Continent has been found in the UK at only two locations, Pitlochry, Perthshire, and in the north-east of England. One explanation is that it arrived in Scotland on red squirrels introduced from Europe in the 19th century. Heavy infestation of fleas and lice can cause ill-health in red squirrels and can be associated with a noticeable hair loss.

A range of predators are known to kill red squirrels, but there is no evidence that any of these has a significant role in the national decline of the species.

1
Goshawk.
2
Fox.
3
Pine marten.

1

2

3

Disease monitoring in most wild animals is patchy but is vital to discover emerging or undetected diseases. This is an area which requires further study.

Fungal infections such as ringworm *Trichopyton* sp. infection have been reported in red squirrels. In addition, both red and grey squirrels can suffer from gut parasitic protozoans, most notably *Eimeria sciurorum,* which causes the potentially fatal disease coccidiosis. Red squirrels also suffer from bacterial infections, but only a few cases have been reported, e.g. *Staphylococcus* eye infection and a *Mycobacterium* infection of a 'pet' red squirrel.

Several viruses have been detected in red and grey squirrels. However, the virus currently considered to be most threatening to red squirrels is the squirrelpox virus (formerly known as parapoxvirus). Squirrelpox disease in red squirrel populations in Britain appears to be linked to the spread of the grey squirrel. The disease was first detected in red squirrels in south Scotland in 2005, coinciding with grey squirrels expanding from a known area of infection in north England. Around 60% of grey squirrels sampled in north England tested positive for antibodies to the virus. Grey squirrels show no outward signs of the disease but it appears to be fatal to red squirrels in most cases. Signs of squirrelpox disease in red squirrels resemble those of myxomatosis in rabbits, with infected animals developing sores and ulcers. This is compounded by secondary bacterial infection on their face, feet and thighs. Red squirrels die within 15 days of the first obvious signs of the disease.

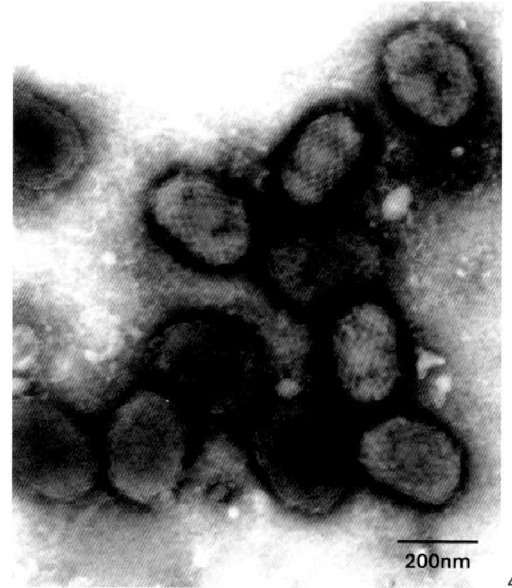

4

The grey squirrel poses the greatest threat to red squirrels in the UK.

Mass migrations

The description of mass migrations in wildlife conjures up images of large herds of wildebeest and other ungulates on the African plains. However, mass migrations are also reported for the red squirrel in Russia. In contrast to large ungulates, squirrels are said to move singly, sometimes out of sight of other squirrels, becoming crowded only where there are large obstacles in their path. The most intense migrations have occurred in late summer and autumn as a response to seed crop failures. One record tells of migrations that lasted for more than two months across a front of 300 kilometres in the 1930s, with squirrels attempting to cross rivers and swim across 1 kilometre of water. Many drowned, while others are said to have clung to rafts, boats and even steamers.

4
Grey squirrels can act as a carrier of squirrelpox, but seldom show any symptoms.
5
Grey squirrel.

5

Threats and conservation

Many factors contribute to red squirrel population declines, including changes in forest habitat, disease or human impacts. However, there is little doubt that the grey squirrel poses the greatest threat and has been responsible for the large-scale decline of the native red squirrel in Britain.

The interaction between red and grey squirrel populations is complex. It is influenced by climate, habitat composition, food availability and landscape factors such as fragmentation of suitable habitat. The impact of the non-native grey squirrel on red squirrels is compounded by their ability to live at significantly higher population densities in deciduous woodland and some mixed woodlands in Britain. This has enabled them to establish more robust, widespread populations which can withstand more difficult conditions and temporary low population numbers. They are also more able to exploit some food resources than red squirrels, showing no effects to natural plant defence compounds (polyphenols) found in acorns which act as digestion inhibitors in the native red squirrel. This gives grey squirrels a considerable advantage over red squirrels in exploiting oak woodlands.

1

There is no evidence that grey squirrels aggressively chase red squirrels, or that they interfere with their mating behaviour. However, grey squirrels are known to pilfer red squirrel food caches potentially depriving red squirrel females of food during critical times of the year.

Grey squirrel competition can result in reduced growth in young squirrels, fewer females producing a second litter in the summer and significantly fewer juvenile red squirrels recruiting into a local population. These combined impacts can lead to a decline in the size of the population and, over time, its extinction.

Whilst the two species inhabit very similar ecological niches, there are subtle differences in their ecology, meaning that targeted action can create circumstances that favour red squirrel survival over grey squirrels. For example, encouraging conifer woodland can reduce grey squirrel density and enable red squirrel populations to persist in the presence of the non-native species.

Also, it is known that, in areas where the squirrelpox virus is present rather than in areas that are disease-free red squirrel populations decline at a much faster rate. Preventing the spread of the disease, by reducing contact between the species, is of paramount importance to red squirrel conservation.

2 

1
Clear felling of woodland results in loss of squirrel habitat.

2
Radio-tracking can be used to show squirrel movements – an important research tool.

Squirrels and people

In medieval times, red squirrels were hunted for their fur, which, along with the fur of fox, pine marten and otter, was used to line cloaks and make warm clothing. Shipping records suggest that skins were imported from Flanders to Scotland for this purpose. However, they have also been used more recently in the ladies fashion industry and, in 1839 alone, over 2,700,000 red squirrel skins were imported to Britain largely to manufacture fur boas (a coil of fur worn around the neck by ladies). Squirrels skins were used in medieval times to line cloaks and make warm clothing.

1

2

1
Squirrel fur was once prized for lining cloaks and for fur boas, but it is no longer used for this purpose.

2
Red squirrels foraging in autumn.

Both red and grey squirrels can cause damage to trees. Grey squirrels, which live at a higher density generally inflict more significant and concentrated damage, but damage can also be recorded in areas with only red squirrels. They do this by stripping the bark to get to the sap-bearing plant tissue beneath with the resulting wound making the tree more susceptible to disease. Damaged trees may have several patches or wounds along the trunk. In some cases the bark can be removed right around the main stem (called 'ring barking'), resulting in the death of the top of the tree as the sap is no longer able to reach the upper branches. This type of damage can ultimately lead to wind-snap or can kill trees if it occurs near the base. Bark-stripping tends to occur in spring or early summer and is generally associated with areas supporting high densities of red squirrels.

3
A tree showing damage which has been caused by squirrels stripping the bark.
4
Rope bridges provide an alternative route for squirrels to cross busy roads.
5
Red squirrels need to stay alert at all times.

3

4

5

1

2 

Squirrels and the law

This section is intended only as a guide to the law. For further details, please refer to the complete copies of the relevant legislation.

Red squirrels

Wild-living red squirrels are protected by their inclusion on Schedules 5 and 6 of the Wildlife and Countryside Act 1981 (as amended). The following provides a brief summary of the provisions of this legislation, under which it is an offence to:

- intentionally kill, injure or take any red squirrel;
- have possession or control of any red squirrel, or any part of, or anything derived from a red squirrel unless it can be proven that it was obtained lawfully;
- damage, destroy or obstruct access to any structure or place used by a red squirrel for shelter or protection;
- disturb a red squirrel while it is occupying a structure or place used for shelter or protection;
- sell, offer or expose for sale, or have for the purpose of sale, any red squirrel;
- publish or cause to be published any advertisement likely to imply that squirrels can, or are intended to be bought or sold;
- use certain indiscriminate methods of taking red squirrels, such as snaring or poisoning.

This protection has been amended and strengthened by the Nature Conservation (Scotland) Act 2004, and anyone perceived to have committed any of the above offences must be able to demonstrate that they have taken 'reasonable precautions' to avoid or minimise the damage to red squirrels.

There is no provision in Scots law, under either the 1981 Act or the 2004 Act, for the legal destruction of red squirrel dreys, for forestry or development purposes. There is, however, provision within the Act for some other activities, that would otherwise be illegal, to be licensed. Scottish Natural Heritage and the Scottish Government share the responsibility for licensing. Purposes for which activities may be licensed under the Wildlife & Countryside Act 1981 include:

1
Red squirrels are protected by law.
2
Young red squirrel.

Responsibility of Scottish Natural Heritage	Responsibility of the Scottish Government
Scientific research or education	Preserving public health or safety
Ringing or marking, or examining any ring or mark on, squirrels	Preventing the spread of disease
Conserving squirrels or introducing them to particular areas	Preventing serious damage to crops, vegetable, fruit, growing timber or any other form of property
Protecting any zoological collection	
Photography	

Red squirrels are also protected under the Wild Mammals (Protection) Act 1996, which makes it illegal to subject them to any wilful act of cruelty or abuse.

Grey squirrels

Grey squirrels are listed on Schedule 9 of the Wildlife and Countryside Act 1981 (as amended). This makes it an offence to release, or allow escape, into the wild any grey squirrel. It is also an offence, by an Order under the Destructive Imported Animals Act 1932, to keep or import grey squirrels except when licensed.

3

4

3
Red squirrel at a feeder.
4
Walking through a forest you can often see squirrel feeding signs such as chewed cones and empty nutshells and seed cases.

Helping squirrels

The red squirrel is included in the Scottish Natural Heritage Species Action Framework (www.snh.org.uk/speciesactionframework/) and a variety of practical actions are underway to conserve red squirrels in Scotland. More information on these can be obtained through SNH (www.snh.org.uk/scottish/species/mammals/squirrels.asp) and the UK Red Squirrel Group (www.snh.org.uk/ukredsquirrelgroup).

Several local groups have been established to enable volunteers to contribute to red squirrel conservation. These form a central group – the Scottish Squirrel Group – which helps to coordinate action within Scotland. People who wish to get involved should contact their local group (see www.snh.org.uk/scottish/species/mammals/squirrels.asp). In addition, sightings of squirrels in areas where they are not seen regularly should be passed to a Local Records Centre, to a local squirrel group, or to SNH. Information on areas where red squirrels have been seen regularly in the past, but not recently, is also of importance to the conservation of the species. Records are vital if we are to be able to monitor the changing fortunes of red and grey squirrels and to implement conservation action accordingly.

1
Red squirrels are adept at their aerial gymnastics.
2
Red squirrels can benefit from feeding boxes.

Names

Scottish names for the squirrel are 'con' 'skurel' 'scurrell' and 'feoragh' in Gaelic.

1

Finding out more

Further reading

Practical techniques for surveying and monitoring squirrels. J. Gurnell, P.W.W. Lurz, & H. Pepper, 2001, Forestry Commission Practice Note No. 11 (http://www.forestry.gov.uk/forestry/library)

Red squirrel *Sciurus vulgaris*. J. Gurnell, P.W.W. Lurz, & E.C. Halliwell, 2008, in: Mammals of the British Isles: Handbook, 4th edition. Mammal Society, Southampton.

Grey squirrel Sciurus carolinensis. J. Gurnell, R.E. Kenward, H. Pepper, & P.W.W. Lurz, 2008, in: Mammals of the British Isles: Handbook, 4th edition. Mammal Society, Southampton.

Late chapters in the history of the squirrel in Great Britain. J.A. Harvie-Brown, 1881, Proceedings of the Royal Physical Society of Edinburgh.

Useful addresses

UK Red Squirrel Action Plan
www.ukbap.org.uk/UKPlans.aspx?ID=565

On-line access to squirrel action plan, strategy, reports and links to local voluntary groups.
www.snh.org.uk/scottish/species/mammals/squirrels.asp

Squirrelweb. Website providing updates on red squirrel research and conservation.
www.squirrelweb.co.uk

Saving Scotland's red squirrels project
www.swt.org.uk/campaigns/scotlands-red-squirrels

Red Squirrels in South Scotland project
www.red-squirrels.org.uk

1
Red squirrels are shy and secretive but are worth the effort when seen in their natural environment.